Printed in the United States of America

ISBN: 9781797479552

Editing by Jennifer Fitzpatrick
Cover & Book design by Roberta Tabb

Roberta Tabb
www.therobertashow.com
www.simplytabbtastic.com

# take care of self

**I'm not self centered, i'm centered within my SELF.**

**My focus goes to what gives me the most out of life. What gives me the most out of life is my FOCUS.**

-Roberta Tabb

# TABBALICIOUS TOC

**Prepare to Prep recommendation list**

- SINGLE SERVE BLENDER OR FOOD PROCESSOR
- JUICER
- WOODEN SKEWERS
- SEALABLE PLASTIC BAGGIES
- 6 32-OUNCE MASON JARS
- 6 16-OUNCE MASON JARS
- 6 24-OUNCE STORAGE CONTAINERS
- 6 1 PINT STORAGE CONTAINERS

# intro

The truth is, your outside is no good if you're feeling bad inside. Your body will only ever be as good as the mind that keeps it in check. Pair these tips with my recipes to beautify the mind and body, inside and out.

Please use Tabbalicious as a guide, or springboard to your new healthy lifestyle. I believe in simple ingredients with simple preparation providing maximum taste. Also, use it as inspiration to get to the SELF you have always wanted to become. The change starts with you, little things, small choices each day over time. Practicing good mental habits and creating good eating habits are the best ways to guarantee success.

**Tabbalicious tips to practice daily**

## START EACH DAY WITH AN AFFIRMATION
whether you find one from your favorite IG (@therobertashow) guru or peruse Pinterest, look for an affirmation that speaks to where you are in life from small to large.

## LEARN SOMETHING
this is as simple as reading an article on one of your favorite topics or researching the calories in your favorite energy bar. You could Pin a recipe or learn a new word definition. Hint* you can find any of these examples in your inbox if you sign up for the right subscription lists.

## ONE SMALL THING
This is my favorite #RobertaRule to live by. I need to feel useful in my own life each day. I can work for 8 hours and still feel useless, however, if I do one thing that gets me closer to a personal goal I can sleep well at night. It could be research, it could be editing photos for my blog or it could writing an email of inquiry. This works! Do for you as you would do for them. During a busy work/social weeks – 5 small things that you've done for yourself start to build up into success over time.

## BE QUIET
For at least ten minutes a day take time to reflect. You could call this praying or meditating. But quiet yourself, your tv, your phone and be still and reflect.

## FIND A HOBBY
Find something simple to make you happy. I plant and grow green things, and I create recipes. You could knit, write stories, paint or restore things. The point of having a hobby is working on something for no other purpose besides the joy of doing it. A hobby shouldn't set you back, or take up too much time, so keep it simple, Simply Tabbtastic.

# raw
# BERTA
prepping the rainbow

# PEAR, APPLE, KALE, COCONUT BOWL

## shopping list

- 3 Pears
- 2 Apples
- 5 cups Kale
- 2 cups Coconut water

## meal prep

Makes 5 smoothies or bowls. Chop pears and apples into 1-inch pieces. Separate ingredients into 5 equal parts. Layer 1 portion of each ingredient into 16-ounce mason jars. Freeze until use, then blend for 60 seconds. Add 1 tbs of water while blending if too thick.

# BLUEBERRY, YOGURT, PINEAPPLE

## shopping list

- 16-ounces Blueberries
- 5 cups plain 0 fat Greek yogurt
- 2 cups fresh Pineapple cubed
- 5 tsp Nutmeg
- 2 Cucumbers cubed

## meal prep

Makes 5 smoothies or bowls. Separate ingredients into 5 equal parts.
Layer 1 portion of each ingredient into 16-ounce mason jars. Freeze until use, then blend for 60 seconds. Add 1 tbsp. of water at a time while blending if too thick.

# BANANA, YOGURT PROTEIN

## shopping list

- 1/2 frozen Banana
- 1 scoop Protein powder
- 1 cup of Greek yogurt
- Ice

## single serving

This is the easiest meal replacement I offer. Literally grab your favorite protein powder, a banana and any kind of fat-free yogurt. You can make this in less than 5 minutes, it's thick, frothy and filling.

## meal prep

Prep this smoothie the same as you would any smoothie for post workout. Freeze ingredients in mason jars until use.

raw-berta

# SWEET BERRY BERTA

## shopping list

- 16-ounces Golden Berries halved
- 16-ounces Strawberries halved
- 5 cups plain 0 fat Greek yogurt
- 2 cups fresh Pineapple cubed

*The stars of this smoothie are the golden berries. Golden berries are tart and sweet, cross between a cherry tomato and strawberry. This smoothie is a beautiful breakfast or post-workout treat. If you can't find golden berries or if they aren't in season, omit or double the strawberries. (this even works for dessert)*

## meal prep

Makes 5 smoothies or bowls. Separate ingredients into 5 equal parts. Layer 1 portion of each ingredient into 16-ounce mason jars. Freeze until use, then blend for 60 seconds. Add 1 tbsp. of water at a time while blending if too thick.

# LEMON GINGER DETOX SIP

## shopping list

- 1 gallon Water
- 1 Lemon
- 5 inches of peeled Ginger root
- 6 mason jars or water bottles

## what to do

1. This potion calls for a bit of prep, it's a truly an infused anomaly.
2. Slice the ginger into pieces and add to a big pot along with the water, bring to a boil and then simmer on low heat for 15 minutes.
3. Remove from heat and let cool. Once cool divide water into six mason jars.
4. Slice the lemon six ways and add to jars, fill with ice and refrigerate.

*(this sip is spicy with a lemon twist – sip in the morning & evening)*

*raw-berta*

# APPLE CINNAMON, GINGER INFUSED WATER

## shopping list

- 1 sliced Gala Apple
- 5 Cinnamon sticks
- 3 inches Ginger

### what to do

Slice the apple and shave the ginger into thin pieces. Separate ingredients into 5 equal shares and place portions into mason jars. Fill the jars with ice and water. Lid and refrigerate for at least 4 hours, lasts for up to a week.

# APPLE PEAR CELERY JUICE

## shopping list

- 4 Green Apples
- 3 Pears
- 4 Celery stalks
- 4 inches of Ginger
- 2 Cucumbers

**what to do**
Wash ingredients well. Juice entire fruit and vegetable – stems, skin & seeds.

**OPTION 1:**
as you juice each ingredient divide juice evenly into 5 16 ounce mason jars

**OPTION 2:**
juice everything all at once and dump into a large container, mix well then evenly distribute into mason jars

## meal prep

5 Mason jars (16 ounce)
repeat recipe x 5 :
freeze until use :
defrost for 20 mins : blend

raw-berta

# TARRAGON, CUCUMBER, INFUSED WATER

## shopping list

- 1 bunch of Tarragon
- 1 Cucumber
- 10 Blackberries

**what to do**
Peel and slice the cucumber
and slice strawberries

Divide ingredients into 5 equal parts
and add to 24 ounce mason jars

MUDDLE FRUIT IN EACH JAR,
juices should mix and fruits and
vegetables should be slightly mashed.
Herbs should be torn for best flavor
and fragrant result.

## meal prep

Separate ingredients into 5 equal
shares and place portions into mason jars.
Fill the jars with ice and water.
Lid and refrigerate for at least 4 hours,
lasts for up to a week.

# CARROT APPLE GINGER JUICE

## shopping list

- 5 Carrots
- 3 Apples
- 4 inches of Ginger
- 2 Cucumbers
- 2 Lemons

**what to do**
Wash ingredients well. Juice entire fruit and vegetable – stems, skin & seeds.

**OPTION 1:**
as you juice each ingredient divide juice evenly into mason 5 jars

**OPTION 2:**
juice everything all at once and dump into a large container, mix well then evenly distribute into mason jars

## meal prep

5 Mason jars (16 ounce)
repeat recipe x 5 :
freeze until use :
defrost for 20 mins :
blend

*raw-berta*

# PINEAPPLE LEMON JUICE

## shopping list

- 1/2  Pineapple
- 3 Cucumbers
- 4 inches of Ginger
- 3 Lemons

**what to do**
Wash ingredients well.
Juice entire fruit and
vegetable – stems, skin
& seeds.

OPTION 1:
as you juice each ingredient
divide juice evenly into mason
5 jars

OPTION 2:
juice everything all at once and
dump into a large container, mix
well then evenly distribute into
mason jars

## meal prep

5 Mason jars (16 ounce)
repeat recipe x 5 :
freeze until use :
defrost for 20 mins :
blend

# ARUGULA CRANBERRY SALAD

### shopping list

- 16-ounces (1 bag) Arugula
- 3 tbsp. Cranberries
- 8 ounces Spinach
- 16 ounces Mushrooms
- 3 tbsp. Blue cheese
- 5 Hard-boiled eggs

*A great way to spice up your salads is to mix bold flavors. Arugula is amongst the more interestingly distinct tasting leafy greens. Mix those with blue cheese and dried cranberries, and you've got magic. This salad is a creative way to add a little character to the average greens. Top with a tbsp. of oil and vinegar or a light balsamic vinaigrette.*

## meal prep

Divide ingredients into 5 equal parts and build salads starting with greens.

Store in airtight containers, salads last for up to 5 days. Great for lunch or dinners.

*raw-berta*

raw-berta

# EDAMAME SALAD

## shopping list

- 1 cup Edamame
- 1 bag (16-ounces) Spinach or Arugula
- 12-ounces Orange Cherry Tomatoes
- 2 tbsp. Parmesan flakes

*Edamame is an excellent source of protein and not just for an appetizer. Edamame adds a unique nutty flavor, and the parmesan marries nicely with the tomatoes creating a perfect balance. This will quickly become one of your favorites. Try this with a light balsamic or just olive oil and a squeeze of lemon juice.*

## meal prep

Separate all ingredients into 5 equal parts. Build salads, starting with spinach and store in airtight containers for up to 6 days.

raw-berta

# QUINOA CHICKPEA BOWL

## shopping list

- 1 16-ounce can Chickpeas
- 5 cups Spinach
- 1/2 juice from 1 Lemon
- 2 tsp. Cumin Spice
- 1/2 tbsp. Coarse Salt
- Cilantro
- 3 stalks Chives
- 2 cups Quinoa (cooked)
- 1/2 large Jalapeño
- 10-ounces Cherry tomatoes

*Obviously, I have a thing for quinoa this year! I pick quinoa over rice easily, not only is it a great low-calorie filler but it's full of the best kinds of nutrients. This recipe is flavor-filled and a tasty option to replace your favorite chipotle bowl for lunch or dinner.*

## what to do

1. Prepare the quinoa as directed, set aside to cool.

2. Finely chop jalapeno and chives and cut tomatoes in half.

3. Rinse chickpeas and pour into a medium-sized bowl, use your fingers to smash half of the chickpeas in the bowl.

4. Once the quinoa has cooled, add to the chickpeas along with the cumin and mix well.

5. In a separate smaller bowl mix the tomatoes, lemon juice, chives, and jalapeno.

6. Combine the veggies mixture with the quinoa-chickpea mix and toss well.

7. Lastly, sprinkle on the salt and as much cilantro leaves as you like.

8. Serve on a bed of spinach leaves.
   Add skinless, boneless grilled chicken for extra protein.

### meal prep

**Portion into 5 equal servings atop a large handful of spinach. Store in air-tight contains for up to 6 days.**

# RAINBOW LETTUCE WRAPS

**shopping list**

- 16-ounces Rice noodles
- 1/2 head Iceberg lettuce
- Cilantro bunch
- 1 Red pepper
- 2 Carrots
- 1/2 small Red cabbage
- 1 Lemon – sliced

Dipping sauce

- 1 tbsp. Peanut butter
- 2 tbsp.  Low sodium Soy sauce
- 1 tbsp. Honey
- 2 tbsp. Vinegar
- 1 tbsp.  Red pepper flakes (optional)
- 2 tbsp. freshly grated Ginger
- 

*I love Asian inspired food, spending time in Thailand only enhanced this preference. Upon returning, I began creating my own inspired recipes. I adapted a straightforward method that has all the Asian flare and none of the fatty unidentifiable ingredients. These wraps are fresh and fabulous for summer grab and go meals.*

## what to do

1.       Prepare rice noodles as directed

2.       Wash and thinly slice cabbage, carrots, and peppers (or use a mandolin to shave)

3.       Wash and carefully separate lettuce leaves, setting aside 10 of the largest leaves

4.       Build the wraps! Start with a palm full of rice noodles. Next fill up the wrap with the veggies, layering in the cabbage and carrots, garnish with as much cilantro as you like.

Sauce – In a small bowl, use a whisk to mix all ingredients together well.

## meal prep

**For meal prep store 2 wraps per air-tight container and portion 1 1/2 tbsp. of sauce into small airtight containers**

*raw-berta*

# berta's
# BAKES

simple baking

# TABBTASTIC TURKEY BALLS

## shopping list

- 2 lbs lean ground Turkey
- 1 small rainbow Peppers
- 1/2 small Onion
- 2 tsp. Salt
- 2 tsp. Pepper
- 2 Eggs
- Grated Ginger
- 2 tbsp. Bread crumbs

Spicy honey glaze
- 2 tbsp. Vinegar
- 2 tbsp. Honey
- 1 tbsp.  Red pepper flakes

*Turkey isn't just for my Tabbtastic Thanksgiving! Actually any time I'm called to use ground meat, I always chose turkey. Even the leanest meat is full of flavor, I love a great big juicy turkey burger, but meatballs are just as good. Here is a bright-juicy recipe for meatballs, perfect for any lunch or dinner.*

## what to do

Preheat the oven to 350 degrees.
In a small bowl whisk together vinegar, honey, and pepper flakes and set aside.

1. Mince (or chop finely) the peppers, ginger and desired amount of onion.

2. In a large bowl mix turkey and eggs together, using a fork or your fingers.

3. Next add the salt, pepper and minced veggies. Mix everything together well.

4. Ingredients should stick together firmly.

5. Create golf ball sized meatballs and place them on a lightly coated heated skillet.

6. Sauté lightly to brown on all sides.

7. Place meatballs on a baking sheet and drizzle glaze over each meatball

8. Bake for 25 minutes, flipping halfway between.

Makes about 15 meatballs.

## meal prep

For meal prep Store 3 per airtight container. Refrigerate for up to 7 days. Pair with roasted veggies or quinoa.

# EASY EGG MUFFINS

## shopping list

- 12 Eggs
- 1/2 cup Goat cheese (or your favorite soft cheese)
- 2 Chive stalks
- 1 medium Tomato
- 1 cup of Kale
- 2 tsp. Salt
- 1 tsp. black Pepper

*Want a perfectly cooked omelet without the hassle of flipping and wondering if all the stuff is going to fall out? I have the perfect solution, takes slightly longer, but a lot less work. These muffins cook perfectly and also reheat easily. I'm not a big fan of eggs, but I consume hoards of them to incorporate protein into daily meals. Hard-boiled eggs have BEEN boring, so these creatively baked egg muffins may become my new staple.*

## what to do

Preheat the oven to 350 degrees. You will need a muffin pan that holds 12 or individual muffin tins and a baking sheet.

1. In a large bowl, crack all the eggs and mix well with a whisk or fork (for low cholesterol, use only the egg whites and add 2 eggs).

2. Next, prep your veggies, chop the chives finely, and cube the tomatoes in half inch pieces.

3. Chop the greens into bite-sized pieces.

4. Add the vegetables to the egg mixture and mix well using a fork.

5. Next, fold the cheese into the egg and veggie mix.

6. Prepare muffin pan lightly coated with olive oil or non-stick spray.

7. Fill a measuring cup to 1/3 with the mixture and pour into the muffin pan or tins. Repeating 12 times.

8. Place the muffin pan or tins on a baking sheet and place in the oven for 25 minutes or until middle is solid.

## meal prep

Remove from tins and store in pairs in the refrigerator for up to 1 week. 30 seconds in the microwave to reheat.

berta's bakes

# QUINOA KALE CAKES

## shopping list

- 1 cup of cooked Quinoa
- 1 cup of shredded Kale
- 1 tsp. Cumin
- 1 tsp. Salt
- 3 Eggs
- 3 Chive stalks

*A good friend of mine served these really delicious premade quinoa cakes while I was visiting. Then I thought „I can do that!" I thought the cakes were a fascinating spin on ingredients I use weekly. The very next day I went home and put a created my version of the recipe. They turned out amazingly, and really appetizing to look at as well.*

## what to do

Preheat oven to 350 degrees

1. Prepare Quinoa as directed, using chicken or vegetable stock to season.

2. Once the quinoa has cooled, in a medium-sized bowl mix in the kale, and chives.

3. In a small bowl beat eggs together, then fold into the quinoa mixture with the cumin and salt.

4. Once well mixed, form the cakes! The easiest way to do this is to use a 1/2 cup sized measuring cup. Packing in the mixture firmly then slamming the cup down on a flat surface to remove the mix. If you don't have one, just form patties with your hand. About the size for the palm of your hand, 3/4 of an inch thick. Make sure the patties are firm (they fall apart easily).

5. Bake for 25 minutes, flipping halfway through.

## meal prep

**Makes 8 patties. Portion 5 ways, store in airtight contains pair with fresh or roasted veggies for lunch or dinner.**

# RED QUINOA STUFFED PEPPERS

## shopping list

- 5 Medium sized rainbow Peppers
- 2 cups Red Quinoa
- 16-ounces Mushrooms
- 1 can Black beans
- 2 tsp. Salt
- 2 tsp. Cumin
- 1 Bouillon cube

*I love a STUFFED anything, ideally stuffed potatoes with lots of cheese and topped with sour cream, enter rainbow peppers. Roasted peppers are great toppers, but also wonderful for filling. I've got a tasty recipe that combines the brightness of bell peppers with a meaty protein for a spicy filling combination.*

## what to do

Preheat oven to 400 degrees

1. Prepare the quinoa accordingly, using the bouillon cubes to season and set aside.

2. Lightly sauté the mushrooms in the olive oil and salt.

3. Drain and rinse the black beans.

4. Mix beans, mushrooms and quinoa together.

5. Next Wash the bell peppers, cut the tops off and scrape the seeds out. Peppers should be completely empty.

6. Lightly coat the outside of the peppers with olive oil.

7. Use a spoon to fill the peppers with the quinoa mixture and place them on a baking sheet

8. Top with a sprinkle of shredded cheese.

9. Bake for 20 minutes

## meal prep

**Remove from oven and store in air tight containers for up to 7 days. Heat in the microwave for 60 seconds.**

# MASHED SWEET POTATOES

## shopping list

- 3 medium-sized Sweet potatoes
- 1 tsp. coarse Salt
- 2 tbsp. Parmesan cheese flakes
- 3 tbsp. Olive oil
- 2 Chive stalks
- Parsley (garnish)

*Sweet potatoes are a healthy go-to. However, the usual twice baked with pepper and salt gets a little boring without all the fat-filled gooey toppings. Here's an easy but interesting recipe that's great for meal prep or just an easy dinner idea.*

## what to do

Preheat oven to 350 degrees.

1. Wash the potatoes thoroughly, then cut them into 1/2 inch slices, discarding the ends (makes about 12).

2. Lay the slices on a lined baking sheet and coat each with a drop of Olive Oil, rubbing to cover the whole surface.

3. Bake the slices for about 30 minutes.

4. While baking, finely chop up the chives and break parsley into pieces.

5. After 30 minutes remove the potatoes from the oven and Set the oven to broil.

6. Next, use a large fork to mash each slice lightly, centers should be soft to touch.

7. Next pile on your toppings and sprinkle oil over the slices and put them back in the oven for about 10 minutes or until cheese is browned.

## meal prep

These reheat excellently, 2 slices per serving, 45 seconds in the microwave is all it takes. Makes about 6 servings. For meal prep, Serve with BUNCHES of sautéed kale, see Simply Tabbtasic for an easy recipe.

berta's bakes

# BERTA'S
# BASIL PIZZA

## shopping list

- 12-16 Basil leaves
- 2 heaping tbsp. of Goat cheese
- 2 tsp. olive oil
- fresh Parsley
- 1.5 tomato
- dried Basil flakes (optional)
- Red pepper flakes (optional)
- 1 Laffa or pita bread (80-200 cal)

*I love bread, and I love cheese; unfortunately, these things work against me in the game of life. The easiest way to assure I'm not doing the most damage to my stomach and my waist-line is to make my own pizza. I make these amazing little pizzas whenever I get the urge to do something bad. Basil and goat cheese are a great combination on any level of extreme tastes.*
*\*note: basil, parsley, and peppers came from my own Harlem garden!*

## what to do

Preheat the oven to 350 degrees

1.  Coat your bread with olive oil and basil flakes, rubbing the surface with fingertips.

2.  Place in the oven for 10 minutes then remove from oven

3.  Layer on the rest of the ingredients starting with the tomatoes however you want. Sprinkle a few drops of olive oil on the top and place in the oven.

4.  Bake for 15 minutes. Cool & EAT!!! Guilt-free! 350 calories or LESS.

## meal prep

Repeat above steps X 5. Cut pizzas in fourths and store in air tight containers. These keep wonderfully, reheat in the microwave for 45 seconds.

# SPINACH-STUFFED CHICKEN

## shopping list

- 3 large Boneless skinless Chicken breasts
- 1 cup chopped fresh Spinach
- 2 tsp. Salt
- 1 tsp. Pepper
- 1 Lemon
- 1 cup Shredded mozzarella cheese
- 2 tbsp. Olive oil

*You all love meat! I get it, you ask, and I deliver. I've trained myself not to require meat mentally, and haven't found the need to consume it daily; however, I'm great at preparing it. That said, look how easy it is to stuff a chicken! For you meat lovers, here's a simple recipe for a seemingly complicated prep.*

## what to do

Preheat the oven to 350 degrees

1. In a bowl mix spinach, salt, pepper, and cheese.

2. Separate mixture into 3 equal portions.

3. Clean the chicken breast, cut fat off any fat and slice lengthwise down the middle leaving about half an inch attached creating a flap.

4. Open the flaps and stuff each breast with spinach mixture

5. Close the flap, use a toothpick to close the flaps if needed

6. Place the stuffed breast on an oil-coated baking pan and sprinkle oil over chicken

7. Bake for 25 minutes

8. Remove from oven and cut breasts in half.

## meal prep

**For meal prep: Store halves in air tight containers paired with fresh or veggies or quinoa**

*berta's bakes*

# BAKED CHEESE TOMATOES

## shopping list

- 3 medium vine Tomatoes (or any tomatoes)
- 1/2 tbsp. Coarse Sea Salt
- 2 tbsp. Parmesan flakes (or shredded gouda cheese)
- 1 tbsp. Olive oil
- Oregano garnish

*Want a pizza that's not a pizza, or a grilled cheese that's not a grilled cheese that won't leave you riddled with guilt and a massive gut? I've got a recipe for breadless grilled cheese, honestly even if you ate the whole recipe for lunch you'd be better off than having one slice of pizza or a whole grilled cheese sandwich. I'm nothing if not resourceful with random leftover ingredients and resourcefulness counts for everything in life. \*carb and calorie saver.*

## what to do

Preheat the oven to 375 degrees or simply use the broil setting

1. Slice the tomatoes as thick as you like, make them sturdy, mine were about half an inch

2. Place tomatoes on foil or a lightly oiled cookie sheet

3. Sprinkle on the cheese layer, then a light salt sprinkle

4. Lastly, drizzle on a little olive oil on each tomato

5. Place in the oven for about 15 minutes or until the cheese has browned lightly. If broiling it should take half the time. Sprinkle on optional oregano

Great for snacking or lunch with fresh avocado.

*berta's bakes*

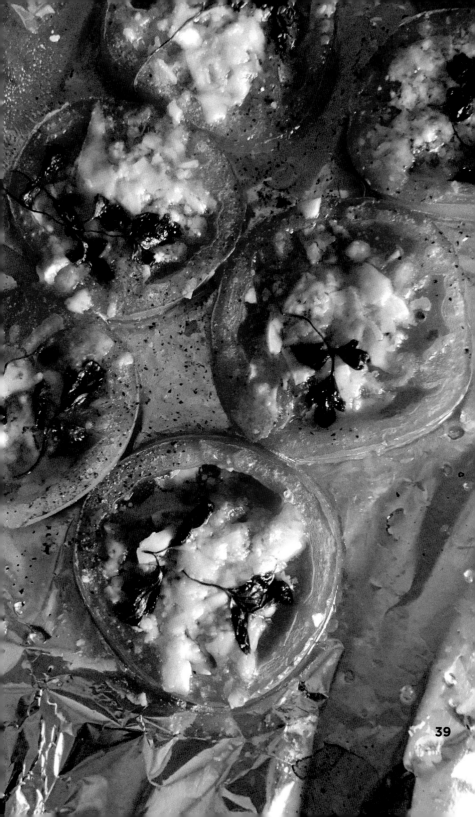

# SIMPLY
# BAKED
# APPLES

## shopping list

- 1 Granny Smith Apple
- 1 tbsp. Brown Sugar
- pinch of Coarse Sea Salt
- 1 tbsp. of Cinnamon or
  The Only French Toast Seasoning You'll Ever Need™
- Grated Ginger

*I've always loved creating something from nothing. As a kid, I spent many weekends with my grandmother, and I had the run of the kitchen. By the time we went grocery shopping there was usually just canned food and random fruits laying around. I learned to make myself sugar infused tasty treats from the fruits and whatever staples I found in the fridge or cabinets. Here is a great alternate apple recipe to one of my favorite childhood snacks.*

## what to do

Preheat the oven to 375.

1. Cut the top and bottom off the apple so that the apple will sit flat on a baking sheet.

2. Place the apple on the baking sheet and top with as much grated ginger as you like.

3. Next, add the brown sugar and cinnamon.

4. Bake for 25 minutes or until sides of apple are soft to touch, sugar should be caramelized on top.

5. Add a pinch of salt and eat!

*berta's bakes*

# EASY BAKED BANANAS

## shopping list

- 1 ripe Banana
- 1 tbsp. Honey
- Basil leaves
- A squeeze of Lemon juice
- 1 tbsp. The only French Toast Seasoning You'll Ever Need™

*I eat a lot of bananas, they are probably my primary source of sugar (which probably means I should give them up). Bananas are my go-to for dessert. Whether it be smeared with peanut butter or frozen \*Nice Cream, they are a valued substitute and a quick sugar fix. This time try baking them, it's like a warm gooey banana split. Great for lazy autumn Saturdays and cold winter nights.*

## what to do

Preheat the oven to 375 degrees.

1. On a baking sheet or aluminum foil, open the banana, but leave it in the peel and lay it open side up. The peel will act as an excellent receptacle for the toppings.

2. Lay a few basil leaves inside the banana peel and drizzle the honey all over the banana.

3. Next, sprinkle the season generously over the banana and squeeze the lemon juice on.

4. Bake for 20 minutes, or when tops are brown, longer for a deeper caramelization.

*berta's bakes*

# PB
# DATE
# COOKIES

## shopping list

- 1 cup  Pitted Dates
- 1 cup  Creamy natural Peanut butter
- 1 tsp. Vanilla
- 1 large Egg
- 2 tsp.  Nutmeg  or The Only French Toast Seasoning
  You'll Ever Need ™

*I'm obsessed with dates. I'm finding all sorts of exciting ways to use dates as a sugar substitute. I came across this recipe and tweaked it slightly to make it Tabbalicious. These tasty little desserts literally took 20 minutes from start to finish. I LOVE cookies, I love peanut butter, and I now love dates, WINS all around. Additional perk – dates are FULL of fiber!*

## what you need
Parchment paper, fork, food processor/blender

## what to do

Preheat oven to 350 degrees.

1. Blend the dates in the food processor, adding 1/2 TBS of water if needed.

2. Once the dates are blended into a paste add all the additional ingredients.

3. Once well mixed, with wet hands form mixture into 1.5 inch balls.

4. Place on baking sheet lined with parchment paper 1 inch apart, then with a wet fork flatten and create a crisscross pattern.

5. Bake for 10 minutes exactly.

6. Cool for a few minutes and ENJOY!

## meal prep
**Seal in an airtight container or zip-lock baggies, 2 a day keeps the sugar urges away! Enjoy & SHARE!**

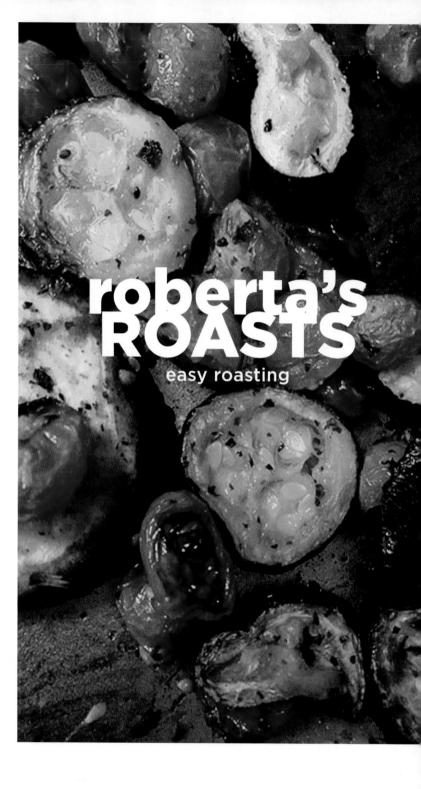

# roberta's ROASTS

easy roasting

# SPICY-SWEET SALMON

### shopping list

- 2 lbs Salmon
- 2 tbsp. Brown Sugar or The Only French Toast Seasoning You'll Ever Need
- 2 tsp Coarse Salt
- 1 tbsp. Olive oil
- 1 Lemon

*Fresh salmon is amongst my favorite fish, but for a long time, it seemed intimidating to prepare myself. I'll tell you it's easier than probably any other meal prep. There are so few steps, and so many options to season lightly it should be a staple when your feeling fishy. Salmon is full of protein and good fats – there is no wrong way to prep this.*

### what to do

Preheat the oven to broil

1. Clean your fish and cut into 2-inch fillets (should make 5 fillets)

2. Lay fillets on a glass or metal baking sheet (aluminum foil works too) an inch apart.

3. Sprinkle brown sugar or TOFTSYEN generously over each piece

4. Drizzle olive oil over lightly then broil for 20-25 minutes.

*try adding a pinch of cayenne pepper for sweet and spicy

## meal prep

Store in 5 airtight containers atop any salad or pair with quinoa or sautéed kale for the perfect lunch or dinner.

48

# ROASTED OKRA

## shopping list

- 16-ounces fresh or frozen Okra sliced into half-inch pieces
- 1 tbsp. Coconut oil or Olive oil
- 1 tbsp. Coarse Salt

*Growing up the mention of okra was always followed by a prompt "EWWWWW!" from my sisters and I. My mom and grandma made something called okra pie (even sounded disgusting) mostly, it was layered okra, white rice, can tomatoes and crisp bacon all baked together like a pie. I actually never really minded the okra slime, as long as it was heavily buttered and salted. Still – okra is green AND slimy, easily a punishment food for children!*

*I have an easy, but KILLER recipe that only requires 3 ingredients. The first time I prepped roasted okra, I ate the entire portion for dinner – guilt-free. This okra is crispy on the outside and warm and chewy on the inside, best of all – there's no slime factor.*

### what to do

Preheat oven to 425 degrees

1. Spread okra evenly on a baking sheet

2. Toss with oil to coat all pieces

3. Sprinkle with half TBS salt

4. Bake for 35-45 minutes tossing at 20 minutes to avoid sticking.

5. Roast until tips are browned.

6. Remove from oven, toss with additional salt.

## meal prep

Portion into 5 servings.
Store in air-tight containers for up to 7 days

# VEGGIE SKEWERS

## shopping list

- **Red pepper**
- **Onions**
- **Zucchini/squash**
- **Mushrooms**
- **Cherry Tomatoes**
- **Coarse Salt (optional)**
- **2 tbsp. Olive oil**
- **10-12 wooden skewers**

*Charring your favorite veggies is always a good idea. The more colors you add, the better snacking you'll have. Veggie kabobs are an excellent idea for grab and go snacking, or you can add them over rice or quinoa for a well-rounded lunch or dinner. Start with 3-5 of your favorite colorful veggies and mix your favorite flavors to create the perfect, simple and tasty combination. Use more or less of whatever your favorites are, you can't do this wrong! My favorite combo is below.*

## What to do

*Preheat the oven to 425 degrees.*

1. *Cut or slice your veggies into bite-sized pieces.*

2. *Create a pattern with your vegetables and repeat twice or until the skewer is filled leaving a 1/2 inch empty on each side.*

3. *Brush olive oil on to coat each piece.*

4. *Lay skewers on a baking sheet or aluminum foil and place in the oven.*

5. *Roast for 30-40 minutes, flipping halfway through. Once peppers start to blister and tips, begin to char your veggies are done. If your vegetables aren't charred, set the oven to broil for 5 minutes!*

6. *Remove from oven and sprinkle on salt.*

*\*Add skinless, boneless chicken breast or Salmon chunks for more protein*

## meal prep

**Leave them on the skewer or portion 2 skewers per container to store for up to 6 days.**

# ROASTED BRUSSELS

## shopping list

- 2lb fresh large Brussels sprouts
- 1 tbsp. + 1 tbsp. Coarse salt
- 2 tbsp. Olive oil

*Brussel sprouts are on trend. Now that we finally know they're tasty, how do we cook them without adding bacon, syrup or butter? The answer is simple – a nice roast and a little salt. Brussel sprouts are a whole mood when prepped tender on the inside and crispy on the outside.*

## what to do

Preheat oven to 425.

1. Rinse Brussel sprouts well

2. Cut the ends of the Brussels sprouts off and discard, cut Brussels in halves or fourths (if larger)

3. Place Brussels in a large bowl and toss with olive oil to coat well.

4. While tossing add 1 TBS of salt.

5. Place evenly on a baking sheet.

6. Roast for 30-35 minutes, flipping every 10 minutes or until tips are browned.

7. Sprinkle additional tbsp. of salt and toss well.

## meal prep

**Split into 5 even portions to store in airtight containers for lunch or dinner.**

# berta
# BITES

simple snacking

# CAYENNE ROASTED PINEAPPLE BITS

## shopping list

- 1 Pineapple
- 1 tbsp. Cayenne pepper
- 2 tsp. salt

*I love heat AND sweet, combine them and its true love. The perfect pineapples are super sweet and pairing it with cayenne pepper is a match made in holy hot hell! I use these spicy pineapples to heat up mmy salads or just as a snack when I'm craving a sweet kick.*
*cayenne pepper is fantastic for boosting your metabolism*

## what to do

Preheat the oven to 425 degrees.

1. Chop the fresh pineapple into cubes about an inch thick and dump into a large bowl.

2. Sprinkle on the cayenne pepper, gently tossing the pineapple so that all the pieces are well coated.

3. Next lay the pineapple on an aluminum foil covered baking sheet or large glass baking pan.

4. Bake for 15 minutes then toss/turn the pineapples, bake 10 more minutes or until the pineapple tips are brown. Sprinkle on salt sparingly.

## meal prep

separate into 5 equal parts and store in zip-lock bags or add directly to your favorite salad prep.

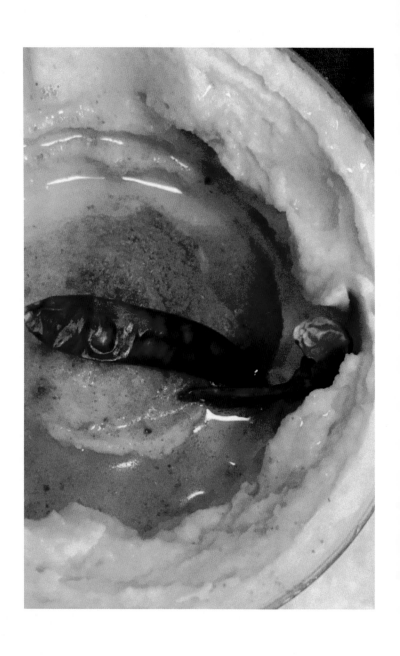

# SPICY
# HUMMUS

## shopping list

- **15 oz Can Chickpeas**
- **2 tbsp. Natural Peanut Butter**
- **1/4 tsp. of Cumin spice**
- **Juice of half a large Lemon**
- **1/4 Cup Olive Oil**
- **2 Cloves Garlic**
- **1 tsp. Salt**
- **3-4 tbsp. liquid from chickpea can**
- **1/4 tsp. Cayenne pepper (or 1 small dried chili)**

*This hummus is addicting! When I realized my famous spinach dip wouldn't last long within my healthy lifestyle, I searched for something else to be known for at potlucks and for holiday appetizers. Hummus works better than you would expect. Smooth and spicy, the kick the spice adds is unexpected and far from store-bought blandness. This recipe is a direct mirror of my personality: healthy and surprisingly sassy!  (add more lemon juice to taper spice, if needed)*

## what to do

1. Drain chickpeas and set drained water aside

2. Place all ingredients in the food processor or blender except the water.

3. Blend until smooth, about 1 minute.

4. Add in water one tablespoon at a time and blend until you achieve your desired thickness.

5. Chill, serve with raw veggies or bake your favorite wraps into pita chips.

### meal prep

**Portion 5 ways and store in mini airtight containers for easy grab-and-go snacks.**

# KRISPY KALE CHIPS

## shopping list

- 2 cups of Spinach or Kale
- 1 tbsp. Coarse salt
- 2 tbsp. Olive oil

Kale chips are a quick and easy snack for any time of the day. If you're missing out on the savory addition to your daily diet, these chips fill the void. Follow the recipe exactly – this is probably the easiest recipe to flop – but totally worthwhile once you get it right! Additionally, you can season these with whatever you like once you get the recipe perfected!

## what to do

Preheat the oven to 250 degrees.

1. Dry the kale in a salad spinner, or set the kale out for a few hours to dry on the kitchen counter.

2. Once the kale is completely DRY, put the kale in a large bowl and sprinkle on the olive oil lightly. Toss with your fingers, lightly coating all the leaves.

3. Lay the kale flat on a baking sheet and lightly sprinkle the salt on.

4. Bake for 25 minutes, start checking around 15 minutes to ensure spinach does not char.

## meal prep

Portion 5 ways and store in mini airtight containers for easy grab-and-go snacks.

# AVOCADO CHOCOLATE NICE CREAM

## shopping list

- 1/2 small ripe Avocado
- 2 tsp Hersheys chocolate powder
- 1 Ripe frozen Banana

*The chocolate version of Berta's banana Nice Cream. The avocado blends the chocolate into a silky-smooth creamy dream. Try this when in the mood for an easy chocolate treat.*

## what to do

1. Chill the avocado.

2. Combine all ingredients in a food processor or blender and blend for 30 seconds. You may need to add a TBS of water if too thick. Blend for 30 more seconds.

3. Be sure the banana and avocado are still cold. The chillier, the thicker, the thicker, the better.

berta's bites

# BLACKBERRY INFUSED CUBES

## shopping list

- Basil
- Lemon
- Blackberries
- Honey

*Infused ice cubes! An effortless and INTERESTING way to stay hydrated. I bought a bunch of ice cube molds for entertaining purposes and thought why not try this quick and easy idea with the stuff I commonly have in my fridge. 4 ingredients create this really gorgeous execution. The best thing about this idea is you can add as much or as little as you want in fruits and herbs. Use these cubes to cool down in the afternoon if you haven't prepped your infused water – or when guests come to visit for brunch or breakfast.*

## what to do

Macerate all the ingredients in a bowl, then stir in water. Then FREEZE until solid. The best thing about this idea is you can add as much or as little as you want in fruits and herbs. Use these cubes to cool down in the afternoon if you haven't prepped your infused water – or when guests come to visit for brunch or breakfast.

*I used large square ice molds, I bought specifically to make Old Fashioneds, what I learned is that a blackberry-lemon bourbon Old fashioned is as good as a regular, if not better!

## spicy Cumin crunch

- 1/2 cup Popcorn kernels
- 2 tbsp. Olive oil
- 2 tsp. Cumin spice
- 2 tsp. fine Salt

## salt & pepper pop

- 1/2 cup Popcorn kernels
- 2 tbsp. Olive oil
- 2 tsp. Black pepper
- 1 tsp. Cayenne pepper
- 3 tsp. fine Salt

## French toast pop

- 1/2 cup Popcorn kernels
- 2 tbsp. Olive oil
- 1 tbsp. The Only French Toast Seasoning You'll Ever Need
- 1 teaspoon fine Salt

# POP CORN

*Popped corn! An easy snack, even if you aren't using the microwave – all you need is a lidded pot and oil! This seems a bit old fashioned but most times, going back to your simple roots garner the best results. Here are a few recipes for whatever your extreme tastes are. Sweet, salty or spicy – popcorn CAN make the perfect light snack if prepared and portioned correctly.*

## what to do

1. *Add the olive oil to a large pot.*

2. *On a stove top turn the flame to high to heat the oil, this should take about 60 seconds.*

3. *Once you see ripples in the oil, add the popcorn kernels to the heated oil. Be sure the kernels are coated, swirling the pot if need be, then place the lid on the pot.*

4. *After about 30 seconds turn the flame down to medium. The Kernels should start to pop after about 30 more seconds.*

5. *Once the kernels begin to pop, carefully shake the lidded pot back and forth to stir the kernels. Place the pot back on the fire and continue to shake every 15 seconds or so.*

6. *Once the kernels slow to pop, pay close attention and once the pops slow to 1 or 2 a second remove from heat.*

7. *Carefully take the lid off the pot. Once the steam has lifted, add the desired seasoning! Toss the popcorn in the pot to coat well.*

## meal prep

**Portion into 5 equal shares and store in air-tight containers or ziplock baggies for daily snacking.**

*berta's bites*

# shopping lists
example weekly meal-prep shopping lists for one

# 30dollars (or less)

| | |
|---|---|
| $2 | 4 lemons |
| $2 | 1 can chickpeas |
| $5 | 2  12-ounces bags of spinach / kale |
| $2 | 1 pint berries |
| $4 | 12-ounces  steel cut oats |
| $3 | 4 sweet potatoes |
| $5 | 16-ounces quinoa |
| $1 | 1 bunch chives |
| $1 | 2 cloves garlic |
| $3 | 10 pita wraps |
| $2 | 1 bag carrots |

**Tabbalicious recipe ideas:**
hummus, quinoa spinach salad, berry-banana smoothies, oatmeal parfait, sweet potato mash

| | |
|---|---|
| $5 | 2 cans salmon |
| $2 | 4 lemons |
| $4 | 1 lb grapes |
| $4 | 16-ounces brown rice |
| $3 | 1 pineapple |
| $5 | 4 Greek yogurts |
| $2 | ginger |
| $4 | 2 16-ounce packages frozen green vegetables (okra, mixed, peas, kale, Brussel sprouts) |

**Tabbalicious recipe ideas:**
salmon patties, roasted veggies, pineapple parfaits, lemon-ginger infused waterinfused water

# 35dollars (or less)

| | |
|---|---|
| $3 | 16-ounce bag of beans (navy, black, pinto) |
| $4 | 1 pack turkey bacon |
| $5 | 2 packs of berries |
| $3 | 3 cucumbers |
| $3 | 1 dozen eggs |
| $4 | 1 lb brown rice |
| $5 | 2 bags spinach |
| $3 | 3 red bell peppers |
| $2 | 2 cans of chickpeas |
| $3 | 4 lemons |

**Tabbalicious recipe ideas:**
spicy hummus and veggies, beans and rice, egg muffins, eggs and bacon, spinach-chickpea salad, veggie stir fry

# 40dollars (or less)

| | |
|---|---|
| $3 | 1 lb Jazmine rice |
| $2 | 2 cans black beans |
| $3 | 1 pineapple |
| $5 | 2 16-ounce bags of spinach or fresh greens |
| $4 | 16-ounces of oats |
| $3 | 4 bananas |
| $3 | dozen eggs |
| $5 | 2 pints  berries |
| $4 | almonds / nuts |
| $6 | 2 lbs skinless chicken breast |
| $3 | 1 jar natural peanut butter |

**Tabbalicious recipe ideas:**
stuffed chicken, rice and beans, oatmeal and fresh berries, sautéed spinach, PB berry-banana smoothies

**TABBALICIOUS**

# shopping lists

example weekly meal-prep shopping lists for one

# 40dollars (or less)

| | |
|---|---|
| $5 | 2 pints berries |
| $4 | 3 lbs apples |
| $3 | cabbage head |
| $3 | carrots |
| $4 | 1/2 gallon soy milk |
| $5 | 12-ounces chia seeds |
| $4 | sugar snap peas / edamame |
| $8 | 2 lbs salmon |
| $3 | 12-ounces mushrooms |
| $3 | 4 Bananas |
| $4 | dates |

**Tabbalicious recipe ideas:**
Broiled salmon, sautéed cabbage and carrots, berry-chia pudding

| | |
|---|---|
| $6 | 2 lbs lean ground turkey |
| $3 | 12 ounces tofu |
| $4 | 5 green apples |
| $3 | 16 ounces of kale |
| $3 | 4 sweet potatoes |
| $2 | 4 bananas |
| $4 | 1 bunch asparagus |
| $5 | 4 squash or zucchini |
| $3 | carrots |
| $5 | 2 avocados |

**Tabbalicious recipe ideas:**
roasted veggies, banana-tofu smoothies, turkey meatballs, sautéed kale

# 45dollars (or less)

| | |
|---|---|
| $8 | 2 lbs of salmon |
| $3 | 16-ounces Brussel sprouts |
| $6 | 1 lb red quinoa |
| $3 | ginger |
| $3 | 1 fresh pineapple |
| $5 | 16-ounces plain Greek yogurt |
| $5 | 2 pints berries |
| $3 | 4 lemons |
| $3 | wheat pitas wraps |
| $4 | vine tomatoes |
| $5 | 2 avocados |

**Tabbalicious recipe ideas:**
Broiled salmon, roasted brussels, avocado mash, lemon-pineapple infused water, pineapple-blueberry parfait, pita chips pudding

# 50dollars (or less)

| | |
|---|---|
| $6 | 2 lbs skinless chicken  breast |
| $6 | 2 lbs lean Ground turkey |
| $3 | dozen eggs |
| $4 | 2 lbs brown rice |
| $4 | 1 lb Broccoli or cauliflower |
| $5 | 2 pints berries |
| $3 | 4 lemons |
| $6 | 16 ounces plain Greek yogurt |
| $3 | Natural Peanut butter |
| $5 | 3 lbs bell peppers |
| $3 | 3 vine tomatoes |
| $3 | 10 pita wraps |
| $5 | olive oil |
| $3 | ginger |
| $3 | 5 bananas |

**Tabbalicious recipe ideas:**
turkey meatballs & brown rice stuffed peppers, grilled chicken wraps, roasted broccoli, PB berry smoothies

*shopping lists*

# low-carb lists

low-carb easy snacking

| | CARBS | FAT | PROTEIN |
|---|---|---|---|
| **SWEET** | | | |
| Blackberries | 5g carbs | 0 fat | 0g protein |
| Watermelon | 8g carbs | 0 fat | 1g protein |
| Kiwi | 10g carbs | 0 fat | 1g protein |
| **SAVORY** | | | |
| Almonds | 6g carbs | 15g fat | 3g protein |
| Rice cake | 7g carbs | 0 fat | 1g protein |
| Zucchini | 6g carbs | .5g fat | 2.5g protein |
| (try veggie skewers - page 51) | | | |
| Almond butter | 3g carbs | 9g fat | 1g protein |
| Pickles | 0g carbs | 0g fat | 0 protein |
| Avocado (1/2) | 3g carbs | 21g fat | 3g protein |
| (try avocado sunshine - Simply Tabbtastic page 43) | | | |
| Salsa | 7g carbs | 0g fat | 1.5 protein |
| Cabbage | 5g carbs | 1g fat | 1g protein |
| (try cabbage steaks Simply Tabbtastic page 42) | | | |
| Tomato | 7g carbs | 0g fat | 1g protein |
| (try baked cheese tomatoes - page 40) | | | |
| **DAIRY** | | | |
| String cheese | 0 carbs | 6g fat | 6g protein |
| 0 fat Greek yogurt | 0 carbs | 0 fat | 13g protein |
| Cheddar cheese slice | 0 carbs | 9g fat | 7g protein |
| Non-fat Cottage Cheese | 6 carbs | 0 fat | 19 g protein |
| (try a berry parfait or smoothie - Simply Tabbtastic page 39) | | | |
| Parmesan cheese | 1g carbs | 8 fat | 6g protein |

*low carb lists*

# low-carb lists
low-carb easy snacking

| | CARBS | FAT | PROTEIN |
|---|---|---|---|

## VEGGIE

| | CARBS | FAT | PROTEIN |
|---|---|---|---|
| Celery | 0 carbs | 0 fat | 0 protein |
| Mushrooms | 2 carbs | 0 fat | 2g protein |
| Green bell Pepper | 9 carbs | 0 fat | 0 protein |
| Cucumber | 5 carbs | 0 fat | 0 protein |
| Kale / spinach chips | 6 carbs | 0 fat | 3g protein |

**(try krispy kale chips - page 58)**

| | | | |
|---|---|---|---|
| Sugar snap peas | 12 carbs | 0 fat | 0 protein |
| Shishito peppers | 4carbs | 0g fat | 1g protein |
| Cauliflower | 7g carbs | .5g fat | 3g protein |

**(try cumin califlower - Simply Tabbtastic page 44)**

| | | | |
|---|---|---|---|
| Olives | 2g carbs | 4g fat | 0 protein |
| Radishes | 2 carbs | 0 fat | 0 protein |

## PROTEIN

| | | | |
|---|---|---|---|
| Hard boiled egg | 0 carbs | 5g fat | 6g protein |

(try deviled eggs)

| | | | |
|---|---|---|---|
| Can albacore Tuna in water | 0 carbs | 0 fat | 13g protein |

**(try Tabb tuna burgers - Simply Tabbtastic page 48)**

| | | | |
|---|---|---|---|
| Beef or turkey jerky | 0 carbs | 13g fat | 22g protein |
| Turkey meatballs | 0 carbs | 9g fat | 22g protein |

**(try Tabbtastic turkey meatballs - page 25)**

| | | | |
|---|---|---|---|
| Can Salmon | 0 carb | 4g fat | 13g protien |

*low carb lists*

## Roberta Rules

### 1. TAKE CARE OF YOURSELF FIRST.

If you aren't your priority first now, you will have nothing worthwhile to give later.

### 2. IF YOU WANT SOMETHING, WORK FOR IT CONSISTENTLY.

Consistency is the only way your success will come and STAY..

### 3. DON'T LET ANYONE WASTE YOUR TIME.

Your time is precious. Even if you're doing nothing by yourself, it's better than wasting time with people you don't like or doing things you hate.

### 4. DON'T LET ANYONE TREAT YOU LESS THAN YOUR WORTH.

The key to getting treated what your worth is first, KNOWING your worth. Then acting your worth by making decisions with your worth in mind.

### 5. Don't expect ANYTHING from ANYONE.

You have to do it for yourself, BY yourself if you expect it to last.

### 6. CLAP FOR YOURSELF.

Reward yourself, don't wait for praise from others.
This is how you self-sustain long-term.

### 7. F**K WHAT ANYONE ELSE THINKS ABOUT YOUR PATH/JOURNEY.

Self-explanatory. Haters gonna hate!

### 8. TEACH PEOPLE HOW TO TREAT YOU.

Never settle and hold yourself to the highest regard.
Don't change your personal rules and say no if you need to, with no explanation.

### 9. DON'T BE A SHITTY PERSON.

Stick to your rules, but don't be offensive if you can help it.

### 10. LIVE – RIGHT NOW.

You will wait for forever if you wait for someone else to give you the life you want to live. START. RIGHT NOW.

97698388R00043